PREFATORY NOTE.

In presenting this, the seventh book of the "1001 Question and Answer Series," we feel that a great want is partially met. It is evident, from the number of inquiries made for such a book, that the works devoted to the subject of Orthography are very limited.

We are also aware that the Authors of the different Grammars devote such a limited space to the subject of Orthoepy and technical Orthography, that both Teacher and Pupil turn away from the subject in disgust.

In preparing this list of questions and answers we have consulted the best authority of the present day, and believe we have gone over the ground in such a way that it will meet the approval of all interested.

The questions and answers on Reading we trust will add to the interest of the book, and only hope that it will be received with as gracious a welcome and hearty approval as the rest of the series.

B.A.H.

CONTENTS.

PAGE.

Letters,

Orthoepy,

Substitutes,

Definitions and Words,

Rules and Terms,

Numerical Values of the Letters,

Capitals and Italics,

Abbreviations,

Accent and Punctuation,

Diacritical Marks,

Prefixes and Suffixes,

Promiscuous Questions,

Reading and Elocution,

LETTERS.

1. *What is Orthography?*
The science and art of the Letters of a language.

2. *Of what does Orthography treat?*
The nature and power of letters, and correct spelling.

3. *From what is the word Orthography derived?*
Two Greek words, signifying "To write right."

4. *What is a Letter?*
A character used to represent an elementary sound, or combination of
  sounds.

5. *What is an Alphabet of a Language?*
A complete list of its letters.

6. *What is the origin of the word Alphabet?*
It is derived from the first two letters of the Greek Alphabet: Alpha and
  Beta.

7. *Where did the Alphabet originate?*
The English comes from the Greek, which was brought by Cadmus from
  Phoenicia, about the year 1490 B.C.

8. *What was the first Alphabet ever used?*
The Hebrew.

9 *How many letters were in the original Alphabet?*
Sixteen.

10. *Where did the other letters originate?*
They have been added since the time of Cadmus, as their use became
  necessary.

11. *What was the last letter added to the English Alphabet?*
W.

12. *Why was it called W?*
On account of it being composed of two u's, or a double u.

13. *How many letters in the English Alphabet?*
Twenty-six.

14. *How many in the Latin Alphabet?*
Twenty-five.

15. *What is the difference between the Latin Alphabet and the English?*
The Latin omits the letter W.

16. *What Alphabet has the greatest number of letters?*
The Chinese.

17. *How many letters in the Chinese Alphabet?*
Over two hundred.

18. *What is a Perfect Alphabet?*
One which contains the same number of letters that it has elementary
    sounds.

19. *Is the English a perfect Alphabet?*
It is not.

20. *How many Elementary sounds in the English Language?*
About forty-three.

21. *What is an Imperfect Alphabet?*
One in which the number of sounds exceeds the number of letters.

22. *What is an Equivocal Alphabet?*
An Imperfect one.

23. *What is an Unequivocal Alphabet?*
Same as Perfect.

24. *Is the English Alphabet Equivocal or Unequivocal?*
Equivocal.

25. *What is a Univocal Alphabet?*
One that has a separate character for each elementary sound.

26. *What is an Alphabetic Language?*
A language in which the characters represent separate articulate sounds.

27. *What is a Phonetic Alphabet?*
One in which there is a separate character for each elementary sound.

28. *Is there any Phonetic Alphabet of the English Language?*
There have been several published, but they are not in general use.

29. *How many letters in the English Phonetic Alphabet?*
Forty-three.

30. *What is the name of a Letter?*
The appellation by which it is known.

31. *What is the difference between a Letter and its Name?*
The letter is the character, and the name is its appellation.

32. *What Letters name themselves?*
The vowels A, E, I, O, and U.

33. *How are the Letters divided?*
Into Vowels and Consonants.

34. *What are Vowels?*
Those letters which represent only pure tones.

35. *Name all the Vowels.*
A, E, I, O, U, and in some situations W and Y.

36. *What is a Consonant?*
A letter that represents an interruption of sound or breath.

37. *Why called Consonants?*
Because they cannot be used alone in a word, but must be connected with a
    Vowel.

38. *How many kinds of Consonants are there?*
Two; single Letters and Combinations.

39. *Name the Consonant letters.*
B, C, D, F, G, H, J, K, L, M, N, P, Q, R, S, T, V, W, X, Y, and Z.

40. *Name the Consonant Combinations.*
Th, Sh, Ch, Zh, Wh, and Ng.

41. *Name the two Orders of the Consonants.*
Mutes and Semi-vowels.

42. *What are Mutes?*
Those letters which admit of no escape of breath while the organs of speech
    are in contact.

43. *Name the Mutes.*
B, D, K, P, T, and C and G hard.

44. *What other term is often applied to the Mutes?*
Close Consonant.

45. *What are Semi-vowels?*
Those letters that admit of an escape of breath while the organs of speech
    are in contact.

46. *Name the Semi-vowels.*
F, H, J, L, M, N, R, S, V, W, X, Y, Z, and C and G soft.

47. *Are the Combinations Mutes or Semi-vowels?*
They are all Semi-vowels.

48. *What letters are called Nasals?*
M, N, and Ng.

49. *What other term is often applied to the Semi-vowels?*
Loose Consonant.

50. *What letters are called Liquids?*
L, M, N, and R.

51. *Why are the Liquids so called?*
Because of their flowing sound, which readily unites with the sound of other letters.

52. *What are Sibilants?*
Letters which have a hissing sound; as, S and Z.

53. *What letter is called the Mute Sibilant?*
The letter X.

54. *What letters represent no sound of their own?*
C, Q, and X.

55. *What are these letters called?*
Redundant letters.

56. *Why are they so named?*
Because they are not necessary for the completion of the Alphabet.

57. *By what letters are the sounds of C represented?*
K and S.

58. *What letters represent the sound of Q?*
Kw.

59. *What letters represent the sound X?*
Ks.

60. *What letters of themselves form words?*
A, I, and O.

61. *Spell all of the Consonants.*

Bee, Cee, Dee, Eff, Gee, Aitch, Jay, Kay, Ell, Em, En, Pee, Kw, Ar, Ess, Tee, Vee, Double-u, Ex, Wy, and Zee.—*Goold Brown.*

62. *What letters are called the Twins?*
Q and U.

63. *Why so called?*
Because Q is always followed by U in English spelling.

64. *Is there any exception to this rule?*
The word LEECLERCQ is sometimes given as an example, but in English it is spelled LEECLERC.

65. *What is meant by style of letters?*
Different type; as, Roman, Script, Italics, etc.

66. *How many forms have letters?*
Two.

67. *What are they?*
Small letters and Capitals.

68. *What are the Natural Divisions of Consonants?*
Subvocals and Aspirates.

69. *What are Subvocals?*
Those Consonants which produce an undertone of voice when their sounds are uttered.

70. *Name the Subvocals.*
B, D, G hard; J and G soft; L, M, N, R, V, W, Y, Z, Zh, and Ng.

71. *What are Aspirates?*
Mere whispers made by the organs of speech and breath.

72. *Name the Aspirates.*
C, F, H, K, P, Q, S, T, X, Ch, Sh, and Wh.

73. *What Combination is both Aspirate and Subvocal?*

Th.

74. *What are Cognate letters?*
Those which are produced by the same organs of speech in a similar
    position.

75. *Give an example of a Cognate letter.*
D is a cognate of T.

76. *What are Quiescent letters?*
Those that are silent.

77. *How many uses have Silent letters?*
Five.

78. *What are they?*
To modify vowels; to modify consonants; to determine signification; to
    determine origin; and to distinguish words of like signification.

79. *What are Explodents?*
Those letters whose sound cannot be prolonged.

80. *Name the Explodents.*
B, D, G, J, P, Q, T, and K.

81. *What are the principle organs of speech?*
Lips, teeth, tongue, and palate.

82. *What is meant by Organical division of the consonants?*
Pertaining to those particular organs used in their pronunciation.

83. *Name the Organical divisions.*
Labials, Dentals, Linguals, and Palatals.

84. *What are Labials?*
Those letters whose sounds are modified by the lips.

85. *Name them.*
B, F, M, P, V, W, and Wh.

86. *What are Dentals?*
Those letters whose sounds are modified by the teeth.

87. *Name them.*
J, S, Z, Ch, Sh, Zh, C and G soft.

88. *What are Linguals?*
Those letters whose sounds are modified by the tongue.

89. *Name them.*
D, L, N, R, T, Y, and Th.

90. *What are Palatals?*
Those letters whose sounds are modified by the palate.

91. *Name them.*
K, Q, X, Ng, C and G hard.

92. *What letters have no Organical classification?*
H, and all the vowels.

93. *What is an Aphthong?*
A silent letter or combination.

94. *How many kinds of Aphthongs?*
Three.

95. *What are they?*
Vowels, Consonants, and Combinations.

96. *What letters are never silent?*
F, J, Q, R, and X.

97. *In what words is V silent?*
Sevennight and twelvemonth.

98. *In what word is Z silent?*
Rendezvous.

99. *What letters are never doubled?*
X and H.

100. *How many words contain all the vowels in regular order?*
Two.

101. *What are they?*
Abstemious and Facetious.

102. *What is a Diphthong?*
Two vowels sounded together in the same syllable.

103. *Name the Diphthongs.*
Ou, Ow, Oi, and Oy.

104. *How many sounds do they represent?*
Two.

105. *What are the sounds called?*
Diphthongal sounds.

106. *How many kinds of Diphthongs are there?*
Two.

107. *What are they?*
Separable and Inseparable.

108. *Which ones are Separable?*
Oi and Oy.

109. *What is an Improper Diphthong?*
The union of two vowels in a syllable, one of which is silent.

110. *By what other name are they known?*
Digraph.

111. *How many Digraphs are there?*
Twenty-five.

112. *Name them.*
Aa, Ae, Ai, Ao, Au, Aw, Ay, Ea, Ee, Ei, Eo, Eu, Ew, Ey, Ie, Oa, Oe, Oi, Oo,
   Ou, Ow, Ua, Ue, Ui, and Uy.

113. *What is a Trigraph?*
A union of three vowels in one syllable, two of which are silent, or all three
   representing one sound.

114. *How many Trigraphs are there?*
Eight.

115. *Name them.*
Awe, Aye, Eau, Eou, Eye, Ieu, Iew, and Uoi.

116. *What is a Tetragraph?*
Union of four vowels in one syllable.

117. *How many Tetragraphs are there?*
One.

118. *What is it?*
Ueue in the word Queue.

119. *May the terms Digraph, etc., be used with the Consonants?*
They may.

120. *Give example of Consonant Digraph.*
Gh, in the word laugh.

121. *Give example of Consonant Trigraph.*
Thr, in the word throw.

122. *Give example of Consonant Tetragraph.*
Phth, in the word phthisic.

123. *What is a regular Triphthong?*
A vowel trigraph in which all three of the vowels are sounded.

124. *Give an example.*

Quoit.

ORTHOEPY.

1. *What is Orthoepy?*
That science which treats of the elementary sounds and the pronunciation of words.

2. *What is Phonology?*
The science of the elementary sounds uttered by the human voice in speech.

3. *What is an Elementary sound?*
One that cannot be divided so as to be represented by two or more letters.

4. *What is Sound?*
A sensation produced on the auditory nerve by the rapid vibratory motion of any elastic substance.

5. *What is the least number of vibrations that will produce an audible sound?*
Sixteen per second.

6. *What is the greatest number that can be heard?*
About forty thousand per second.

7. *What is Voice?*
Sound produced by the vocal chords.

8. *What is an Articulate sound?*
One made by the organs of speech and used in language.

9. *What is a Vocal sound?*
One that is modified but not obstructed by the articulatory organs.

10. *What is a simple Vocal sound?*
One made without any change in the position of the articulatory organs during its emission.

11. *What is a Coalescent?*
An articulate sound that always precedes and unites with a vocal.

12. *What is a Guttural sound?*
One that is modified by the soft palate.

13. *What are Unarticulate sounds?*
The sounds of the vowels.

14. *How many Elementary sounds do the vowels represent?*
Fifteen.

15. *How many do the Consonants represent?*
Eighteen.

16. *How many do the Combinations represent?*
Seven.

17. *How many do the Diphthongs represent?*
Only one, as oi and oy only repeat sounds already represented by a and i.

18. *How many sounds has A?*
Five.

19. *What are they?*
Long, Short, Medial, Flat, and Broad.

20. *How many sounds has E?*
Two.

21. *What are they?*
Long and Short.

22. *How many sounds has I?*
Two.

23. *What are they?*
Long and Short.

24. *How many sounds has O?*
Three.

25. *What are they?*
Long, Short, and Slender.

26. *How many sounds has U?*
Three.

27. *What are they?*
Long, Short, and Medial.

28. *How many sounds has B?*
One; as heard in the word babe.

29. *How many sounds has C?*
None that may be properly called its own.

30. *How many sounds has D?*
One; as heard in the word did.

31. *How many sounds has F?*
One; as heard in the word flew.

32. *How many sounds has G?*
Two; as heard in the words go and age.

33. *How many sounds has H?*
One; as heard in the word high.

34. *How many sounds has J?*
None of its own, but represents one; the sound of G.

35. *How many sounds has K?*
One; as heard in the word key.

36. *How many sounds has L?*
One; as heard in the word lily.

37. *How many sounds has M?*
One; as heard in the word money.

38. *How many sounds has N?*
One; as heard in the word nat.

39. *How many sounds has P?*
One; as heard in the word pie.

40. *How many sounds has R?*
One; as heard in the word roar. (REM.—Some authors give r three sounds.)

41. *How many sounds has S?*
One; as heard in the word same.

42. *How many sounds has T?*
One; as heard in the word tight.

43. *How many sounds has V?*
One; as heard in the word view.

44. *How many sounds has W?*
One; as heard in the word we.

45. *How many sounds has X?*
None of its own, as it is a redundant letter.

46. *How many sounds has Z?*
One; as heard in the word ooze.

47. *How many sounds has Th?*
Two; as heard in the words thigh and the.

48. *How many sounds has Ch?*
One; as heard in the word church.

49. *How many sounds has Sh?*
One; as heard in the word ash.

50. *How many sounds has Zh?*
One obscurely; represented by *si* in such words as fusion, *zi* in glazier.

51. *How many sounds has Wh?*
One; as heard in the word what.

52. *How many sounds has Ng?*
One; as heard in the word sing.

53. *What are regular sounds?*
The long sounds of the letters.

SUBSTITUTES.

1. *What is a Substitute?*
A letter representing a sound usually represented by another.

2. *What are Equivalent letters?*
Letters representing the same sound.

3. *What properties do Substitutes assume?*
The properties of the letter whose sound it represents.

4. *How many Substitutes has a long?*
Four.

5. *What are they?*
E in tete; *ei* in feint; *ey* in they; and *ao* in gaol.

6. *How many Substitutes has a middle?*
Two.

7. *What are they?*
E in there; and *ei* in heir.

8. *How many Substitutes has a broad?*
Two.

9. *What are they?*
O in cord; and *ou* in sought.

10. *How many Substitutes has e long?*
Three.

11. *What are they?*
I in marine; *ie* in fiend; and *ay* in quay.

12. *How many Substitutes has e short?*

Two.

13. *What are they?*
A in says; and *u* in bury.

14. *How many Substitutes has i long?*
Two.

15. *What are they?*
Y in chyme; and *oi* in choir.

16. *How many Substitutes has i short?*
Six.

17. *What are they?*
Y in hymn; *e* in England; *u* in busy; *o* in women; *ee* in been; and *ai* in
    captain.

18. *How many Substitutes has o long?*
Two.

19. *What are they?*
Eau in beau; and *ew* in sew.

20. *How many Substitutes has o short?*
One.

21. *What is it?*
A in what.

22. *How many Substitutes has u long?*
One.

23. *What is it?*
Ew in new.

24. *How many Substitutes has u short?*
Three.

25. *What are they?*
E in her; *i* in sir; and *o* in son.

26. *How many Substitutes has u medial?*
One.

27. *What is it?*
O in wolf.

28. *How many Substitutes has F?*
Two.

29. *What are they?*
Gh in laugh; and *ph* in philosophy.

30. *How many Substitutes has J?*
Three.

31. *What are they?*
G in rage; *di* in soldier; and *d* in verdure.

32. *How many Substitutes has S?*
Two.

33. *What are they?*
C soft, as in central; and *z* in quartz.

34. *How many Substitutes has T?*
One.

35. *What is it?*
Ed final, after any aspirate except t.

36. *How many Substitutes has V?*
One.

37. *What is it?*
F in of.

38. *How many Substitutes has W?*
One.

39. *What is it?*
U in quick.

40. *How many Substitutes has X?*
One.

41. *What is it?*
Ks in exist.

42. *How many Substitutes has Y?*
One.

43. *What is it?*
I in alien.

44. *How many Substitutes has Z?*
Three.

45. *What are they?*
S in was; *c* in suffice; and *x* in xebec.

46. *How many Substitutes has Ch?*
Two.

47. *What are they?*
Ti in question; and *t* in nature.

48. *How many Substitutes has Sh?*
Six.

49. *What are they?*
Ce in ocean; *ci* in social; *si* in mansion; *ti* in motion; *ch* in chaise; and *s* in
     sugar.

50. *How many Substitutes has Zh?*
Four.

51. *What are they?*
Si in fusion; *zi* in brazier; *z* in azure; and *s* in rasure.

52. *How many substitutes has Ng?*
One.

53. *What is it?*
N generally before palate sounds; as, conquer, etc.

54. *What letters have no Substitutes?*
B, D, G, H, L, M, N, P, and R.

55. *What combinations have no Substitutes?*
Th and Wh.

56. *Why is X never doubled?*
It already represents the sounds of K and S.

57. *What letter ends no English word?*
J.

DEFINITIONS AND WORDS.

1. *What is Language?*
Any method for the communication of thought and feeling.

2. *What is Natural Language?*
Instinctive methods of communicating thought or feeling.

3. *What is Artificial Language?*
That which must be learned before it can be used.

4. *Is the English Language natural or artificial?*
Artificial.

5. *How many kinds of Artificial Language?*
Two.

6. *What are they.*
Spoken and written.

7. *What is Spoken Language?*
That produced by the vocal organs.

8. *What is Written Language?*
Any method of communicating thought or feeling by the use of written or printed characters.

9. *What are the messengers of thought?*
Sentences.

10. *What is a Sentence?*
An assemblage of words conveying a thought.

11. *What is a Word?*
A sign of an idea.

12. What is Lexicology?
That science which treats of the meaning of words.

13. What is Etymology?
That science which treats of the origin and derivation of words.

14. What is Orthogeny?
That science which treats of the classification of words into parts of speech.

15. What is Syntax?
That science which treats of the relation and connection of words in the construction of a sentence.

16. What is Prosody?
That science which treats of punctuation and the laws of versification.

17. Of what is a word composed?
A syllable or combination of syllables.

18. What is a Syllable?
A letter or letters uttered by a single impulse of the voice.

19. What is the essential part of a syllable?
A vowel.

20. Can there be a syllable without it containing a vowel sound?
There cannot.

21. What is Syllabication?
That branch of etymology which treats of the division of words into syllables.

22. How many methods of Syllabication are there?
Two.

23. What are they?
English and American.

24. What is the object of the English method?

To separate words into their elementary parts without regard to pronunciation; as, a-tom.

25. *What is the object of the American method?*
To indicate the proper pronunciation by separating affixes from the roots.

26. *What is a word of one syllable called?*
A monosyllable.

27. *What is a word of two syllables called?*
A dissyllable.

28. *What is a word of three syllables called?*
A trisyllable.

29. *What is a word of more than three syllables called?*
A polysyllable.

30. *What is the Ultimate syllable of a word?*
The last syllable.

31. *What is the Penultimate syllable?*
Next to the last syllable in a word.

32. *What is the Antepenultimate syllable?*
The last syllable but two in a word.

33. *What is the Preantepenultimate syllable?*
The last syllable but three in a word.

34. *What other way may the syllables be described?*
In their numerical order; as, first, second, etc.

35. *How many syllables can a word have?*
As many as it has vowels or diphthongs sounded.

36. *How many words in the English language?*
About one hundred and twenty thousand.

37. *How are words divided in reference to form?*
Into simple and compound.

38. *How are they divided in reference to origin?*
Into primitive and derivative.

39. *What is a Simple word?*
One that is not composed of two or more whole words.

40. *What is a Compound word?*
One that is composed of two or more distinct words.

41. *What is a Primitive word?*
One in no way derived from another in the same language.

42. *What is a Radical word?*
Same as primitive.

43. *What is a Derivative word?*
One formed by joining to a primitive some letter or letters to modify its
    meaning.

44. *What is Analysis?*
Separating a word or syllable into its elements or parts.

45. *What is Synthesis?*
The process of combining elements to form syllables and words.

46. *What is the Base of a Compound word?*
That word representing the fundamental idea.

47. *What is the Modifier in a Compound word?*
That word which describes the other.

48. *What is the Base of a Derivative word?*
The primitive from which it is derived.

49. *What is the Modifier in a Derivative word?*
The affix.

50. *What is an Affix?*
That part of a derivative word attached to the root.

51. *How many Root words in the English language?*
Over one thousand.

52. *What is a Prefix?*
That part of a derivative word placed before the root.

53. *What is a Postfix?*
That part of a derivative word placed after the root.

54. *What is a Suffix?*
Same as a postfix.

55. *What are Affixes?*
Prefixes and postfixes together are called affixes.

56. *How many kinds of Derivatives are there?*
Two.

57. *What are they?*
Regular and irregular.

58. *What is a Regular derivative?*
One that is formed by the addition of affixes without changing the letters in
     the primitive part (except final *e* silent).

59. *What is an Irregular derivative?*
One in which the letters of the primitive part are changed.

60. *In using Affixes, what rule should be observed?*
The affix and root should be from the same language.

61. *Is the same rule to be observed in forming Compound words?*
It is.

62. *What is a Mongrel compound word?*
One formed contrary to the rule.

Benjamin Adams Hathaway

63. *Give an example.*
Cable-graph and cable-gram.

64. *What are Barbarisms?*
Same as mongrel.

65. *When use the hyphen in Compound words?*
When they are not permanently compounded.

66. *What is an Obsolete word?*
One gone out of date.

RULES AND TERMS.

1. *What is Spelling?*
A distinct expression of the letters or sounds of a word in their proper order.

2. *How many kinds of Spelling?*
Two.

3. *What are they?*
Orthographic and Phonic.

4. *What is Orthographic spelling?*
An expression of the letters of a written or printed word in their proper order.

5. *What is Phonic spelling?*
An expression of the elementary sounds of a word in their proper order, according to established usage.

6. *What is meant by good usage?*
The usage, or custom, of the best speakers and writers of the times.

7. *How do we know when we have spelled a word correctly?*
By reference to the Dictionary?

8. *What is a Lexicographer?*
An author of a dictionary.

9. *Can we spell by Rules?*
We cannot.

10. *Why?*
Because there are too many exceptions.

11. *What makes a rule in Orthography?*
Whenever a letter is silent, or usually so, a rule is formed.

12. *Why is c placed before r in acre, massacre, etc.?*
To preserve the hard sound of c.

13. *What is the rule for Digraphs?*
A digraph must have one vowel silent.

14. *Give rule for E final.*
E final is silent when another vowel precedes it in the same syllable.

15. *What effect does final E have on the preceding vowel?*
It usually preserves its long sound.

16. *When is B silent?*
Before *t*, or after *m*, in the same syllable.

17. *When is C silent?*
Before *k* in the same syllable; also, before *z*, *l*, or
t, in a few words.

18. *When is D silent?*
Before *g* in the same syllable.

19. *When is G silent?*
Before *m* or *n* in the same syllable.

20. *When is H silent?*
After *g* or *r* in the same syllable; and *h* final after a vowel is always silent;
    also, in a few words after *t*, and initial in a few words.

21. *When is L silent?*
After *a* when followed by *f*, *m*, *k*, or *v*, except in the word valve; also,
    before *d* in could, etc.

22. *When is M silent?*
Before *n* in a few words.

23. *When is N silent?*
Final after *l* or *m*.

24. *When is P silent?*
Initial before *n, s,* or *t.*

25. *When is S silent?*
In a few irregular words; as, *isle, puisne, viscount, corps,* etc.

26. *When is T silent?*
Before *ch* in the same syllable; also, in *Christmas, eclat, mortgage,* etc.

27. *When is V silent?*
In two words only—*Sevennight* and *Twelvemonth.*

28. *When is W silent?*
Before *r* in the same syllable also, in *whoop, sword, two,* etc.

29. *When is Gh silent?*
After *i* in the same syllable; also, after *au* and *ou* in some words.

30. *When is Ch silent?*
In a few words; as, *drachm, yacht,* etc.

31. *When is Z silent?*
In one word only—*Rendezvous.*

32. *What letters are never silent?*
F, J, Q, and R.

33. *What is meant by Antecedent part of a syllable?*
That part before the vowel.

34. *What is the Consequent part of a syllable?*
That part which follows the vowel.

35. *How many words end in Ceed?*
Three.

36. *What are they?*
Exceed, proceed, and succeed.

37. *How many of the English words are derived from the Latin?*
About, three-fourths.

38. *What Language is called "Our mother tongue?"*
Anglo-Saxon.

39. *From what language do we get most of our Scientific terms?*
The Greek.

40. *How many English words begin with* IN *as a prefix?*
Two hundred and fifty.

41. *How many begin with im?*
Seventy-five.

42. *How many begin with un?*
About two thousand.

43. *Were final E not silent, what would be the result?*
Another syllable would be formed.

44. *When is final E dropped in spelling?*
Before vowel terminations mostly.

45. *Why is the final E retained in such words as changeable and traceable?*
To preserve the soft sound of the c or g.

46. *In the words fleeing, seeing, etc., why retain both Es?*
To determine the proper meaning of the word.

47 *What is a Figure of orthography?*
Any departure from the ordinary spelling of a word.

48. *How many Figures are there?*
Two.

49 *What are they?*
Archaism and Mimesis.

50. *What is Archaism?*
The spelling of a word according to ancient usage.

51. *What is Mimesis?*
The spelling of a word in imitation of a false pronunciation.

52. *When is i used as a consonant?*
When followed by a vowel in the same syllable; as in alien, etc.

53. *When is y final changed to e?*
Before the suffix ous; as in beauteous.

54. *When is y final changed to i?*
Before the suffix ful; as in beautiful.

55. *What is a Redundant prefix?*
One that does not change the signification of the root; as, *a* in the word adry.

56. *When is ie changed to y?*
Before the ending *ing*.

57. *When use the digraph ei in spelling?*
Ei follows c soft, and begins words.

58. *When use ie in spelling?*
Ie follows consonants (except c soft), and ends words.

59. *In changing the word hoe to hoeing, why retain the e?*
To preserve its signification.

60. *What is the origin of the suffix less?*
Anglo-Saxon.

61. *What is the origin of the word English?*
It is derived from the word Angles.

1001 Questions and Answers on Orthography and Reading

Benjamin Adams Hathaway

Benjamin Adams Hathaway

1. *What is meant by the Numerical value of letters?*
Its value as a numeral used in the notation of different languages.

2. *Have all the letters Numerical value?*
All except J, U, W, and Y.

3. *What is the Numerical value of A?*
500.

4. *By whom used?*
The ancient European Nations.

5. *What is the Numerical value of B?*
300.

6. *By whom used?*
The Romans.

7. *What is the Numerical value of C?*
100 in the Roman notation.

8. *What is the Numerical value of D?*
500 in the Roman notation.

9. *What is the Numerical value of E?*
5.

10. *By whom used?*
The ancient Greeks.

11. *What is the Numerical value of F?*
40 in some of the Ancient notations; 80 in the Arabian; and 10,000 in the
        Armenian.

12. *What is the Numerical value of G?*
400.

13. *By whom used?*

The Latins.

14. *What is the Numerical value of H?*
100 in the Greek notation; and 200 in the Latin.

15. *What is the Numerical value of I?*
1 in the Roman notation; and 100 in some of the Ancient notations.

16. *What is the Numerical value of K?*
20 in the Greek notation; and 60 in the Semitic.

17. *Give the Numerical values of L.*
50 in Roman, and 30 in Semitic notation.

18. *What are the Numerical values of M?*
As a Roman numeral, 1,000; Greek and Hebrew, 40.

19. *What is the value of N as a Numeral?*
In the Greek notation, 50; Roman, 90; and by some other, 900.

20. *What is the Numerical value of O?*
70 in the Greek; and 11 in the Ancient Latins.

21. *What is the Numerical value of P?*
In the Greek notation, 5; in the Latin, 80; and in the Roman, by some authors, 7, by one, 100, and by still another, 400.

22. *As a Numeral, what is the value of Q?*
500.

23. *By whom used?*
Several of the Ancient Nations of Europe.

24. *What is the Numerical value of R?*
80

25. *By whom used?*
The ancient Romans.

26. *What is the Numerical value of S?*
7

27. *By whom used?*
The Ancients.

28. *Give the values of T as a Numeral.*
300 in the Greek notation; in the Latin, 160.

29. *What is the Numerical value of V?*
5 in the Roman notation.

30. *What are the values of X as a Numeral?*
In the Roman, 10; in the Greek, 60.

31. *What are the Numerical values of Z?*
7 in the Greek notation; and 2,000 in the Roman.

32. *Why have J, U, W, and Y no Numerical values?*
Because they have been introduced into the Alphabet since the Science of
   Arithmetical Notation was invented.

33. *What effect does it have on the value of a letter to draw a line above it?*
In most cases it increases its value a thousand times.

34. *Is a line ever drawn beneath a letter for the same purpose?*
In some instances it is.

35. *What effect does it have on a letter as a numeral to repeat it?*
Repeats its value as often as it is repeated.

CAPITALS AND ITALICS.

1. *What is a Capital letter?*
A large letter.

2. *What is an Italic letter?*
A form of oblique letters derived from the Italians.

3. *What is Rule 1 for the use of Capitals?*
Title pages and headings of chapters should be entirely in capitals.

4. *Give Rule 2.*
The first word of every book, tract, essay, letter, etc., should begin with a capital.

5. *Give Rule 3.*
The first word of every sentence should begin with a capital.

6. *Give Rule 4.*
Clauses separately numbered should begin with a capital.

7. *Give Rule 5.*
The first word after an interrogation point should usually begin with a capital.

8. *Give Rule 6.*
The first word of a clause, or sentence, given as an example, should begin with a capital.

9. *Give Rule 7.*
In quoting a title of a book, each important word of the title should begin with a capital.

10. *Give Rule 8.*
First word of a direct question should begin with a capital.

11. *Give Rule 9.*
The first word of a direct quotation should begin with a capital.

12. *Give Rule 10.*
All letters used as numerals should be written or printed in capitals.

13. *Give Rule 11.*
The pronoun I should always be a capital.

14. *Give Rule 12.*
The vocative particle O should always be a capital.

15. *Give Rule 13.*
The first word of every line of poetry should begin with a capital.

16. *Give one exception to Rule 13.*
In humorous poetry, when a word is divided at the end of a line, the detached syllable at the beginning of the next line should begin with a small letter.

17. *Give Rule 14.*
All names and titles of the Deity should begin with a capital.

18. *Give Rule 15.*
All proper names should begin with a capital.

19. *Give Rule 16.*
All words derived from proper nouns should begin with a capital.

20. *Give Rule 17.*
Titles of honor and distinction should begin with capitals.

21. *Give Rule 18.*
The words father, mother, sister, brother, aunt, etc., when followed by a proper noun, should always begin with a capital.

22. *Give Rule 19.*
All words referring to the Bible should begin with a capital.

23. *Give Rule 20.*
All proper adjectives should begin with a capital.

24. *Give Rule 21.*
The names of famous events, historical eras, noted documents, etc., should
    begin with a capital.

25. *What establishes a rule for Capitals?*
Good usage, or custom.

26. *Give Rule 1 for the use of Italics.*
Words for emphasis should be printed in italics.

27. *Give Rule 2.*
Names of books, poems, etc., are usually printed in italics.

28. *Give Rule 3.*
Words from foreign languages are printed in italics.

29. *Give Rule 4.*
Words in the Bible supplied by the translators are printed in italics.

30. *How are written words marked that are to be printed in Capitals?*
By underscoring the words with two lines.

31. *How are written words marked that are to be printed in Italics?*
By underscoring the words with one line.

32. *When use the Interjection O?*
The letter O is a vocative particle, and should always be used before nouns
    or pronouns in the absolute case by direct address.—[*Ridpath.*]

33. *When use Oh?*
In all cases where it is not followed by nouns, or pronouns, in the vocative
    case.—[*Ridpath.*]

ABBREVIATIONS.

1. *What is an abbreviation?*
One or more of the letters of a word standing for the whole word.

2. *What is the signification of A.C.S.?*
American Colonization Society.

3. *Give meaning A.B.C.F.M.*
American Board of Commissioners for Foreign Missions.

4. *What is the signification AAA.?*
Amalgamation.

5. *What is the signification of Ang.-Sax.?*
Anglo-Saxon.

6. *Give signification of A.T.*
Arch-Treasurer.

7. *What is the signification of C.A.S.?*
Fellow of the Connecticut Academy.

8. *What is the signification of C.C.?*
County Court, or County Commissioner.

9. *What is the meaning of D.C.L.?*
Doctor of Civil Law.

10. *What is the signification of D.M.?*
Doctor of Music.

11. *What is the signification of A.U.C.?*
In the year of the city.

12. *What is the meaning of F.E.S.?*

Fellow of the Entomological Society.

13. *What is the signification of H.R.I.P.?*
Here rests in peace.

14. *What is the signification of L.C.J.?*
Lord Chief Justice.

15. *What is the signification of N.u.?*
Name unknown.

16. *What is the signification of P.a.?*
Participial adjective.

17. *What is the signification of P.v.?*
Post village.

18. *What is the signification of Qy.?*
Query.

19. *What is the signification of Ro.?*
Righthand page.

20. *What is the signification S.C.L.?*
Student of the Civil Law.

21. *What is the signification of S.R.I.?*
Holy Roman Empire.

22. *What is the signification of S.J.C.?*
Supreme Judicial Court.

23. *What is the signification of U.S.S.?*
United States Ship.

24. *What does U.K. signify?*
United Kingdom.

25. *What does V.R. signify?*

Queen Victoria.

26. *What does V.G. signify?*
For example.

27. *What does Xt. signify?*
Christ.

28. *What does Xmas. signify?*
Christmas.

29. *What is the signification of Y.B.?*
Year Book.

30. *What is the signification of Zoöl.?*
Zoölogy.

31. *What does Yt. signify?*
That.

32. *What is the signification of S.T.P.?*
Doctor of Divinity.

ACCENT AND PUNCTUATION.

1. Why is a word divided into syllables?
For the purpose of showing their proper pronunciation and etymological composition.

2. What is Accent?
A greater stress of voice placed on one syllable of a word than the others.

3. What kind of words have no accent?
Monosyllables.

4. Why?
Accent implies comparison, and there can be no comparison with one syllable.

5. How many kinds of accent?
Common, Emphatic, and Discriminating.

6. What is common accent?
Ordinary accent of spelling.

7. How many kinds of common accent?
Two.

8. What are they?
Primary and secondary.

9. What is primary accent?
The principal accent.

10. What is secondary accent?
The partial accent.

11. What kind of accent is essential to every word of more than one syllable?

Primary.

12. *How close can primary and secondary accent come together?*
Not closer than two syllables.

13. *How many primary accents can one word have?*
Only one.

14. *How many secondary accents can a word have?*
Two.

15. *In case of two secondary accents, where are they placed?*
On the first and third.

16. *In case of two secondary, where is the primary accent?*
On the last but two.

17. *Do the primary and secondary ever change places?*
They do.

18. *In words of two syllables, where is the accent?*
Usually on the first.

19. *In trisyllables, what syllable is accented?*
Usually the first.

20. *Are there any exceptions?*
There are.

21. *In polysyllables, where is the accent?*
On the antepenult usually.

22. *In all words ending in ation, where is the accent?*
On the syllable next to the last.

23. *What is Emphatic accent?*
Accent used for emphatic distinction.

24. *Have monosyllables any accent?*

They have sometimes an emphatic, or poetic.

25. *What is Discriminating accent?*
That used to determine parts of speech.

26, *Give some examples.*
Au'gust, Au-gust'; Reb'el, Re-bel'.

27, *What is Punctuation?*
The use of certain characters to aid the reader in determining the thought of
the writer.

28. *How many kinds of punctuation are there?*
Four.

29. *What are they?*
Rhetorical, Etymological, for Reference, and for the Printer.

30. *What is Rhetorical punctuation?*
That used for rhetorical effect.

31. *What is Etymological punctuation?*
That used in Orthography and Orthoepy.

32. *What is Reference punctuation?*
That used to refer the reader to the margin of the page.

33. *What is punctuation for the Printer?*
That used by the writer to inform the printer the kind of type to use.

34. *What are the principal Etymological points?*
Apostrophe, Caret, Dieresis, Macron, Breve, Tilde, Grave Accent, Acute
Accent, Circumflex Accent, Hyphen, and Period.

35. *What is the use of the Apostrophe?*
To indicate the omission of a letter, or letters, of a word.

36. *What letter is omitted in the word o'clock?*
The letter f.

37. *What is the use of the Caret?*
To correct an error of omission.

38. *Is the Caret used in printed copy or manuscript?*
In manuscript.

39. *For what is the Dieresis used?*
To separate two vowels which would otherwise form a diphthong.

40. *Give an example of the use of the Dieresis.*
Zoölogy, and Diëresis.

41. *What is the use of the Macron?*
To mark the long quantity of syllables.

42. *What is a long syllable?*
One in which the vowel has the long sound.

43. *What is the use of the Breve?*
To mark the short quantity of syllables.

44. *What is a short syllable?*
One in which the vowel has the short sound.

45. *What kind of a mark is the Tilde?*
A Spanish mark.

46. *How many uses has the Tilde?*
Two.

47. *What are they?*
Placed over *n* it gives the sound of *ny* as, in cañon. In English it indicates
    certain sounds of the vowels.

48. *How many accent marks are there?*
Three.

49. *What are they?*
Grave, Acute, and Circumflex.

50. *What is the use of the Grave accent?*
To mark the falling inflection.

51. *What is the use of the Acute accent?*
To mark the primary accent, and the rising inflection.

52. *What is the use of the Circumflex?*
To mark the peculiar inflection of the voice in the pronunciation of a word.

53. *How many uses has the Hyphen?*
Three.

54. *What are they?*
To separate the parts of a compound word; to separate a word into syllables; and to divide a word at the end of a line.

55. *When should the Hyphen be used in a compound word?*
When the word has not become permanently compounded.

56. *When use the Dieresis instead of the Hyphen?*
When the syllables are divided by the hyphen, there is no hyphen used between the vowels of the digraph.

57. *What is the use of the Period?*
To denote an abbreviation.

58. *Are there any other uses of the Period?*
There are.

59. *Where else is the Period used?*
In Rhetorical punctuation.

60. *Name the points used in Reference punctuation.*
Asterisk, Obelisk, Parallels, Section, Paragraph, and Index.

61. *Are these marks ever doubled?*
They are.

62. *Are Letters ever used for reference?*

They are.

DIACRITICAL MARKS.

1. What are Diacritical Marks?
Characters indicating the different sounds of letters.

2. Name the Diacritical Marks.
Macron, Breve, Dieresis, Semi-Dieresis, Caret, Tilde, Cedilla, and the
inverted T.

3. Make the Diacritical Marks in the order named:
(‾); (˘); (¨); (·); (ˇ); (~); (˛); (ˏ).

4. What does the Macron indicate?
Over a vowel, its long sound; under e, the sound of a, long; across c, the
sound of k; over g, the hard sound; across th, the subvocal sound,
and over oo, the long sound.

5. What are the uses of the Breve?
Over vowels, it indicates their short sound, and over oo, its short sound.

6. What does the Dieresis indicate?
Over a, its Italian sound; under a, its broad sound; over i, the sound of e,
long; under u, when preceded by r, makes it equivalent to o, Italian.

7. What is the use of the Semi-Dieresis?
Over a, gives it the medium sound; under a, the sound of o, short; over o,
the sound of u, short; under o, the Italian sound; over g, the soft
sound; and under u, the sound of Italian o.

8. Where is the Cedilla used?
Under c, to give it the sound of s.

9. What is the use of the Caret as a Diacritical Mark?
Over a, it indicates the flat sound; over e, the sound of a, flat; over u, the
sound of e, in her.

10. *Where is the Tilde used?*

Over n in Spanish words it indicates that the sound of y immediately
follows. It is also used over e in such words as her, and over i in sir,
etc.

11. *What is the use of the inverted ˳?*

Under s, it gives it the sound of z; under x, it gives the sound of gz.

12. *Give some words illustrating the use of the Macron.*

Māte, bēam, fīne, bōat, tūbe, rōōd, ḡo, and prey.

13. *Give words showing the use of the Breve.*

Măt, sĕt, lŏt, tŭb, and fŏŏt.

14. *Illustrate the use of the Dieresis.*

Cär, polïce, fạlling, and trụe.

15. *Give words showing the use of the Semi-Dieresis.*

Mȧsk, whạt, mȯney, ġin, wọlf, and bụsh.

16. *Illustrate the use of the Caret.*

Fâir, thêre, sûrge, and sometimes over o as in stôrm.

17. *Give words showing the use of the Tilde.*

Mẽrge and cañon.

18. *Illustrate the use of the Cedilla.*

Çell and çhaise.

19. *Give some words showing the use of the inverted t.*

Was̹ and ex̹ist.

20. *Are there any other names for the inverted t?*

It has been given different names by different authors.

21. *What are they?*

"The Perpendicular," "Suspended Macron," etc.

22. *Is the letter y ever marked by Diacritical Marks?*

It is, sometimes.

23. *What marks are used for y?*
Macron and Breve.

24. *Give examples where y is marked with the Macron.*
Spȳ, slȳ, stȳ, etc.

25. *Give example where y is marked with the Breve.*
Hўmn.

26. *What mark is used to cancel silent letters?*
Short bar, similar to the Macron.

PREFIXES AND SUFFIXES.

1. What is the signification of A as a Prefix?
On, in, at, to, or towards.

2. Is A as a prefix ever redundant?
It is.

3. Give examples.
Adry and ameliorate.

4. What does the prefix Ab signify?
From.

5. What does Ab signify?
Away from.

6. What is the signification of Ante?
Before.

7. Name all the prefixes meaning To.
Ad, ac, af, ag, al, an, ap, ar, and at.

8. What does Anti signify?
Against.

9. What does Bis signify?
Twice.

10. What other prefix means the same?
Dis, from the Greek.

11. What does Be signify?
Upon.

12. What does Circum signify?

Around, as circumscribe.

13. *What is the meaning of Cis?*
On this side, as cisalpine.

14. *What prefixes signify With?*
Con, com, co, col, and cor.

15. *What prefixes signify Against?*
Contra and counter.

16. *What does Di signify?*
Two, as ditone.

17. *What prefixes signify Out of, or From?*
E, and ex.

18. *What does Dys signify?*
Ill, or difficult, as dysentery and dyspepsia.

19. *What does Enter signify?*
Between or among.

20. *What does Epi signify?*
On, as epitaph; during, as ephemeral.

21. *What prefix signifies Equal?*
Equi, as equidistant.

22. *What does Extra signify?*
Beyond, as extraordinary.

23. *What is the signification of Eu?*
Well, or agreeable, as euphony.

24. *What does Gain signify?*
Against, as gainsay.

25. *What is the signification of Hex?*

Six, as Hexagon.

26. *What does Hyper signify?*
Over, as hypercriticism.

27. *What does Hypo signify?*
Under, or beneath, as hypotenuse and hypocrite.

28. *What prefixes signify Not or In?*
In, im, il, and ir.

29. *What is the signification of Inter?*
In the midst of, or between, as intellect and intermarry.

30. *What does Intra signify?*
Within, or on the inside of.

31. *What other prefix means the same as Intra?*
Intro.

32. *What is the signification of Juxta?*
Joined to, or next, as juxtaposition.

33. *What does Mal signify?*
Bad, as malpractice and maladministration.

34. *What is the signification of Meta?*
In the middle, after, and with.

35. *What does Mis signify?*
Amiss, or wrong, as misapply and mishap.

36. *What is the signification of Mono?*
One, as monotheistic.

37. *What prefixes signify Many?*
Multi and poly, as multiform and polysyllable.

38. *What does Non signify?*

Not, as nonsense, nonessential, etc.

39. *What other prefixes signify Not?*
Neg, as in negative, and ne, as in nefarious.

40. *What does Ob signify?*
In the way of, as obstruct.

41. *What does Oct signify?*
Eight, as octagon.

42. *What does Omni signify?*
All, or complete, as omnipresent.

43. *What is the signification of Out?*
Beyond, as outlaw, outbid, outbalance, etc.

44. *What does Over signify?*
Above, as overseer, overreach, etc.

45. *What does Ovi signify?*
An egg, as oviform.

46. *What does Para signify?*
Beside, as parallel, paragraph, etc.

47. *What is the signification of Pene?*
Almost, as peninsula—almost an island.

48. *What does Per signify?*
Through, or by, as permit, perchance, etc.

49. *What does Peri signify?*
Around, as perimeter, periosteum.

50. *What does Pleni signify?*
Completeness, or full, as plenitude, etc.

51. *What does Post signify?*

After, or backwards, as postfix, and postpone.

52. *What does Pre signify?*
Before, as prefer, prefix, etc.

53. *What is the signification of Preter?*
Beyond, as preternatural.

54. *What is the signification of Pro?*
Before, forth, and for.

55. *What does Pros signify?*
To, as proselyte.

56. *What is the signification of Proto?*
First, as protocol, protoplasm, etc.

57. *What does Quad signify?*
Four, as quadrangle, etc.

58. *What does Re signify?*
Back, or again, as react, recollect, etc.

59. *What prefixes signify Right?*
Rect and Recti.

60. *What does Retro signify?*
Backwards, as retrospect and retrograde.

61. *What does Se signify?*
By itself, as separate, seclude, etc.

62. *What prefixes signify Half?*
Semi, demi, and hemi, as semicircle, demitone, and hemisphere.

63. *What does Sine signify?*
Without, as sinecure.

64. *What does Stereo signify?*

Solid, as stereotype.

65. *What does Sub signify?*
Under, or inferior, as subterranean and subordinate.

66. *What does Super signify?*
Over, above, or beyond, as supernatural, etc.

67. *What does Suf signify?*
Less or after, as suffix, etc.

68. *What does Supra signify?*
Same as Super.

69. *What does Sur signify?*
More than, as surcharge.

70. *What prefixes signify Together?*
Syn, sy, syl, and sym, as in syntax, system, syllable, and symbol.

71. *What does Trans signify?*
Beyond, across, and again, as transalpine, transatlantic, and transform.

72. *What does Tra signify?*
Across, as traverse.

73. *What is the signification of Tri?*
Three, as trisyllable, triangle, etc.

74. *What does Ultra signify?*
Beyond, as ultramarine.

75. *What does Un signify?*
Not, as unhappy, unable, etc.

76. *What is the signification of Under?*
Below, as undercurrent, underrate, etc.

77. *What does Ve signify?*

No or not, as vehement.

78. *What does Vice signify?*
Instead of, as Vice-President.

79. *What does With signify?*
Against or back, as withstand, withdraw.

80. *What other signification has With in some words?*
Near, as within; together, as withal, etc.

81. *What suffixes signify "able to be"?*
Able, ible, and ile, as curable, audible, and visible.

82. *What suffixes signify rank, or office?*
Acy, ate, ric; dom, and ship, as in curacy, pontificate, bishopric, kingdom,
    and clerkship.

83. *What is the signification of Age?*
Act of, as marriage, passage, etc.

84. *Has the suffix Age any other signification?*
From the Latin ago, it means collection.

85. *What does An signify?*
One who, or the person who acts, as equestrian, pedestrian, etc.

86. *What does Ana signify?*
A collection of memorable sayings, as Franklinana—the sayings of
    Franklin.

87. *What does Ant signify?*
Being, and has the force of ing, as dominant, verdant, etc.

88. *What is the signification of the suffix Art?*
One who, as braggart.

89. *What does Ary signify?*
Place where, or place which, as library, aviary, etc.

90. *What does Ate signify?*
Full of, or abundance, as desolate, passionate, etc.

91. *What is the signification of Celli?*
Little, as vermicelli, etc.

92. *What other suffixes also signify Little?*
Cle, cule, el, en, kin, let, ot, ling, ock, and ie.

93. *What does Ene signify?*
Belonging to, as terrene, etc.

94. *What is the signification of Eous?*
Full of, as beauteous, etc.

95. *What does Ed signify?*
When added to a verb it signifies did, as played; but to a participle, was, as completed.

96. *What is the signification of Er?*
More or often, as brighter, glimmer, etc.

97. *What does Erly signify?*
Direction of, as northerly.

98. *What does Es signify?*
More than one, as foxes, etc.

99. *What does Escent signify?*
Growing or becoming, as convalescent.

100. *What does Esque signify?*
Belonging to, or like, as picturesque, etc.

101. *What does Ess signify?*
Feminine when added to nouns, as tigress.

102. *What does Est signify?*
Greatest or least, as largest, smallest, etc.

103. *What does Head signify?*
State or nature, as Godhead.

104. *What does Ics signify?*
Things relating to, as optics, etc.

105. *What does Ides signify?*
Resemblance, as alkaloides, etc.

106. *What is the signification of Im?*
More than one, as cherubim.

107. *What does Ina signify?*
Feminine, as Czarina.

108. *What does Ing signify?*
Continuing, as singing, etc.

109. *What is the signification of Ior?*
More, as superior.

110. *What does Ique signify?*
Belonging to, as antique.

111. *What is the signification of Ish?*
Like, as boyish, girlish, etc.

112. *What does Isk signify?*
Little, as asterisk, etc.

113. *What does Ite signify?*
That which, as appetite.

114. *What does Ive signify?*
Able to do, as adhesive, etc.

115. *What does Ion signify?*
State or act, as location.

116. *What does Ism signify?*
Doctrine, as Calvinism, etc.

117. *What does Ix signify?*
Feminine of nouns, as testatrix.

118. *What does Kin signify?*
A son of, or little, as lambkin.

119. *What does Kind signify?*
Race, as mankind.

120. *What does Less signify?*
Without, as guiltless, breathless, etc.

121. *What does Ling signify?*
Young, as duckling, etc.

122. *What does Ly signify?*
Like, or in a manner, as manly, calmly, etc.

123. *What does Most signify?*
Greatest or furthest, as hindmost.

124. *What does Ment signify?*
State or act, as settlement, judgment, etc.

125. *What does Ness signify?*
The quality of, or state of, as whiteness, etc.

126. *What does Ock signify?*
Small or young, as hillock, bullock, etc.

127. *What does Oid signify?*
Likeness, as spheroid, etc.

128. *What does Or signify?*
One who, as actor, director, etc.

129. *What does Ory signify?*
Having the quality of, as vibratory, etc.

130. *What does On signify?*
Large, as million, etc.

131. *What does Ous signify?*
Having the quality of, as solicitous.

132. *What does Ot signify?*
Little, as idiot.

133. *What does Re signify?*
Same as *Er,* as it is another form of it.

134. *What does Red signify?*
Those who, as kindred, etc.

135. *What is the signification of Ress?*
Feminine of nouns, as instructress.

136. *What does Ric signify?*
Office of, as bishopric.

137. *What does Ry signify?*
Place where, or things collectively.

138. *What does Se signify?*
To make, as cleanse.

139. *What does San signify?*
The person who, as partisan, etc.

140. *What does Ship signify?*
The condition, as professorship.

141. *What does Some signify?*
Full, as quarrelsome.

142. *What does Ster signify?*
The person who, as teamster.

143. *What does Teen signify?*
Ten to be added, as fourteen.

144. *What is the signification of Tude?*
The state of being, as similitude.

145. *What does Ty signify?*
To multiply into, as seventy, forty, etc.

146. *What does Ude signify?*
Same as *Tude*, the state of being.

147. *What does Ule signify?*
Little, as globule.

148. *What does Ward signify?*
Direction of, as eastward, etc.

149. *What does Ways signify?*
Manner, as crossways, lengthways, etc.

150. *What does the suffix Y signify?*
Plenty, as smoky; also abounding in, as wealthy.

151. *Are there any exceptions to the meaning of the foregoing Prefixes and Postfixes?*
There are some, and therefore great judgment must be exercised in applying them to the analysis of words.

152. *What is meant by the term "Good Bye"?*
God be with you.

153. *What does the suffix Ster signify?*
Feminine, as spinster.

PROMISCUOUS QUESTIONS.

1. *Is A the first letter of all written alphabets?*
All but one, the Abyssinian.

2. *What number is A in the Abyssinian alphabet?*
The thirteenth.

3. *Is double A ever written together as a word?*
It is, as a proper noun.

4. *What is Aa the name of?*
About forty small rivers in Europe.—*Cyclopedia.*

5. *Is B the second letter of all alphabets?*
All except the Ethiopic.

6. *What number is B in the Ethiopic?*
Ninth.

7. *Give a word in which P has the sound of B.*
Cupboard.

8. *What letter is the Sonorous counterpart of T?*
The letter D.—*Cyclopedia.*

9. *Give the Periodic changes of the English language.*
Saxon, Semi-Saxon, Old English, Middle English, and Modern English.

10. *Give date of "Saxon period."*
Previous to 1150 A.D.

11. *Give date of "Semi-Saxon period."*
1150 to 1250.

12. *Give date of "Old English period."*

1250 to 1350.

13. *Give date of "Middle English period."*
1350 to 1550.

14. *Give date of "Modern English period."*
Time since 1550.

15. *What constitutes a Period in Language?*
Any great change in the Literature of a People.

16. *What causes these changes?*
Mostly national invasion.

17. *What is assimilation of Consonants?*
When an aspirate and subvocal comes together, it is necessary to change the sound of one or the other, to make the combination pronounceable.

18. *What is meant by an Element of Speech?*
An indivisible portion of language.

19. *What is a Sonant sound?*
One uttered with intonated or resonant breath.

20. *In changing the word traffic to trafficked, why supply the letter k?*
To preserve the proper sound of c.

21. *Under what condition is a consonant never doubled at the end of a word?*
When immediately following a diphthong.—*Webster.*

22. *When is C followed by K in spelling?*
Words ending with the sound of k, and in which c follows the vowel.

23. *Give some examples.*
Back, black, fleck, etc.

24. *Are there any exceptions?*
There are, as sac, arc, etc.

25. *Why is the word Humbugged spelt with two g's?*
To prevent sounding the g like j.

26. *Give some words spelled differently in the U.S. and in England.*
Woolen—woollen, honor—honour, etc.

27. *When do words, ending in double e, drop one e on taking an additional syllable?*
When the suffix begins with e.

28. *Why?*
To prevent three e's coming together.

29. *Does pluralizing a word ever change the accent?*
Sometimes it does.

30. *Give an example.*
An'tipode—Antip'odes.

31. *In such words as Defense, which is correct, se or ce for the termination?*
Se, because the s belongs to the words from which they are derived.— *Webster.*

32. *Should words of English origin end in ise or ize?*
Ize; same as those from the Greek.

33. *Are there any exceptions to these rules?*
There are; as advertise, from English, etc.

34. *Are the words ox, calf, sheep, and pig of French or Saxon origin?*
Saxon.

35. *From what language do the words beef, veal, mutton, and pork come?*
The Norman-French.

36. *What is a Lexicon?*
A Dictionary.

37. *What is an irregular sound?*

Sound of a Redundant letter.

38. *How are words divided as regards Specie?*
Primitive and Derivative.

39. *How may the meaning of a word be changed?*
By accent; as Aug'ust, August'.

40. *What is an irregular derivative?*
One in which the letters of the root are changed in forming the derivative.

41. *What is Pronunciation?*
The distinct utterance of the sounds of a word.

42. *What are the significant parts of a word?*
Root, prefix, and suffix.

43. *How are words divided as to variety?*
Italic, Roman, Old English, etc.

44. *Name some compound word in which both parts retain their own accent.*
Writ'ing-mas'ter.

45. *Name some word in which one part loses its accent.*
Gentle-manly.

46. *Can all the vowels form syllables themselves?*
All except W.

47. *When has R a rough sound?*
When it begins a word.

48. *How are words distinguished?*
By their forms and uses.

49. *Why do Consonants ever unite?*
To form complex sounds: as rr in Burr.

50. *From what language are most words derived that end in less?*
Anglo-Saxon.

51. *Is Z the last letter of all alphabets?*
All except the Greek, and Hebrew.

52. *What is its place in the Greek alphabet?*
Sixth.

53. *What is its place in the Hebrew?*
Seventh.

54. *What letter is the sonorous counterpart of S?*
The letter Z.—*Cyclopedia.*

55. *What is spelling of Z in England?*
Zed, and also Izzard.

56. *What language has two letters representing the sound of Z?*
The Russian.

57. *When was the letter W first used?*
About the end of the Seventh Century.

58. *What changes the sound of a vowel from long to short?*
The absence of the accent.

59. *In what situation is gh always silent?*
After i in the same syllable.

60. *How many words of two syllables are changed from nouns to verbs by accent?*
About eighty.

61. *What word contains a consonant Tetragraph?*
Phthisic.

62. *What is Philology?*
The science of language.

63. *When is ue final, silent?*
After g and q; as fatigue and oblique.

64. *What are the elements of spoken language?*
Vocal and articulate sounds.

65. *What are Hybrid words?*
Mongrel compounds.

66. *What is Terminology?*
A treatise on technicalities.

READING AND ELOCUTION.

Benjamin Adams Hathaway

1. *What is Reading?*
Silent perusal or distinct utterance of thought and feeling, as seen expressed
      in written language.

2. *How many kinds of Reading are there?*
Two.

3. *What are they?*
Silent and Audible.

4. *What is Silent Reading?*
The perusal of Language without utterance.

5. *What is Audible Reading?*
The utterance of thought and feeling, as seen expressed in written
      Language.

6. *What is Elocution?*
The science and art of the delivery of composition.

7. *How many kinds of Delivery are there?*
Three.

8. *What are they?*
Speaking, Declamation, and Oratory.

9. *What is Speaking?*
The utterance of thought and feeling without reference to the written page.

10. *What is Declamation?*
The delivery of another's composition.

11. *What is Oratory?*
The delivery of one's own composition.

12. *How many kinds of Oratory are there?*
Two.

13. *What are they?*
Prepared and Extempore.

14. *What is Prepared oratory?*
That which has been studied previous to delivery.

15. *What is Extempore oratory?*
That which is accomplished simultaneously with the delivery.

16. *What is Vocal Culture?*
The training of the organs of speech for effective delivery.

17. *What should be the primary object in Audible reading?*
To convey to the hearer the ideas and sentiments of the writer.

18. *In order to accomplish this, what should the Reader do?*
Endeavor to make the feelings and sentiments of the writer his own.

19. *What are some of the essential qualities of a good Reader?*
To read slowly, observe the pauses, give proper inflections, read distinctly, and with expression.

20. *What is Enunciation?*
The utterance of words.

21. *Under how many Divisions should the subject of reading be treated?*
Six.

22. *What are they?*
Articulation, Inflection, Accent, Emphasis, the Voice, and Gesture.

23. *What is Articulation?*
Distinct utterance of the elementary sounds, and of the combinations.

24. *Name four common faults in Articulation.*
Omitting an unaccented vocal, dropping the final sound, sounding incorrectly an unaccented vowel, and omitting syllables.

25. *What is Inflection?*

Sliding of the voice upward or downward.

26. *How many kinds of Inflection are there?*
Two.

27. *What are they?*
Rising and falling.

28. *What is the Rising inflection?*
An upward slide of the voice.

29. *What is the Falling inflection?*
A downward slide of the voice.

30. *Are the rising and falling inflections both ever given to the same sound?*
They are.

31. *How is such inflection marked?*
By the Circumflex.

32. *How many kinds of Circumflex?*
Two.

33. *What are they?*
Rising and falling.

34. *What is the Rising Circumflex?*
The sliding of the voice downward and then upward on the same sound.

35. *What is the Falling Circumflex?*
The sliding of the voice upward and then downward on the same sound.

36. *What is a Monotone?*
Reading without sliding the voice either upward or downward.

37. *Give Rule 1 for falling inflection.*
Propositions which make complete sense require the falling inflection.

38. *Does Emphasis ever reverse this rule?*

It does sometimes.

39. *Give Rule 2.*
Emphasis generally requires the falling inflection.

40. *Where the sense is dependent, what inflection is generally used?*
The rising.

41. *Does Emphasis ever affect this rule?*
Relative emphasis sometimes reverses it.

42. *What kind of inflection should be used at the end of an interrogative sentence?*
Falling, if it cannot be answered by yes or no.

43. *Negative sentences require what kind of inflection?*
Rising.

44. *Does Emphasis ever affect this rule?*
It does; often reversing it.

45. *Imperative sentences have what inflection?*
Usually the falling.

46. *What kind of words require opposite inflection?*
Words or members expressing antithesis or contrast.

47. *What is a Series?*
A number of particulars following one another in the same construction.

48. *How many kinds of Series?*
Two.

49. *What are they?*
Commencing and Concluding.

50. *What is a Commencing Series?*
One that commences a sentence.

51. *What is a Concluding Series?*
One that concludes a sentence.

52. *What inflection is given to the members of a commencing series?*
The rising.

53. *What inflection is given to the members of a concluding series?*
The falling.

54. *Are there any exceptions to these rules?*
There are.

55. *What causes the exceptions?*
Emphasis.

56. *What is a Parenthesis in reading?*
A sentence, or clause, set off by curves from the context.

57. *How should the Parenthesis be read?*
In a lower tone and more rapidly.

58. *What is the use of the Circumflex?*
To express irony, or sarcasm.

59. *What meaning is always suggested by the Circumflex?*
Doubtful or double meaning.

60. *What is the use of the Monotones?*
To produce an effect in grave and solemn subjects.

61. *What is Accent in reading?*
Increase of force on certain syllables of a word.

62. *Give an example of Emphatic accent.*
This corrup'tion must put on in'terruption.

63. *What does Pitch signify?*
The place in the musical scale on which an element is sounded.

64. *What is Force?*
That property of the voice which relates to loudness of sound.

65. *How many different kinds of Force?*
Five.

66. *What are they?*
Suppressed, subdued, ordinary, energetic, and vehement.

67. *To what does Stress relate?*
Different modes of applying force.

68. *How many kinds of Stress?*
Three.

69. *What are they?*
Expulsive, Explosive, and Vanishing.

70. *What is meant by Quantity?*
Length of time the voice dwells on a word.

71. *What is Quality?*
That property which relates to the kind of voice.

72. *What is Movement?*
The degree of rapidity with which the voice moves from one word to
    another.

73. *How many kinds of Movement?*
Six.

74. *What are they?*
Very slow, slow, moderate, lively, rapid, and very rapid.

75. *What does Expression comprehend?*
The practical application of all the principles of reading and elocution.

76. *What is Cadence?*

The natural dropping of the voice at the end of a sentence, denoting completeness of thought.

77. *What is a Rhetorical pause?*
A suspension of the voice for rhetorical effect.

78. *What is Emphasis?*
Giving force and energy to certain words.

79. *How many kinds of Emphasis?*
Two.

80. *What are they?*
Absolute and relative.

81. *What is Absolute emphasis?*
Emphasis made without any contrast with other words.

82. *What is Relative emphasis?*
Emphasis used where there is antithesis either expressed or implied.

83. *Is a whole Phrase ever made emphatic?*
It is often.

84. *For what purpose?*
To give it great force.

85. *What is the Emphatic pause?*
Pause made for emphasis.

86. *What is Antithesis?*
Two or more words opposed to each other in meaning.

87. *What is a Climax?*
A series of particulars increasing in importance to the last.

88. *What is Anti-climax?*
A series of particulars decreasing in importance to the last.

89. *What is meant by Transition?*
Any sudden change in reading.

90. *What is Emphatic repetition?*
Words repeated for emphasis.

91. *What is an Interrogation?*
A statement, or assertion, put in the form of a question.

92. *What is an Exclamation?*
A statement denoting strong emotions.

93. *What is Personation?*
One person imitating the actions and manners of some other person or persons.

94. *How many kinds of style in reading?*
Five.

95. *What are they?*
Description, Argument, Narration, Persuasion, Exhortation.

96. *What should be characteristic of the Descriptive style?*
The Speaker should use the same manner that he would if he were actually describing the thing spoken of.

97. *What should be characteristic of the Argumentative style?*
Directness and earnestness.

98. *What should characterize the Narrative?*
The Reader should proceed as though relating his own experience.

99. *What the Persuasive?*
Those tones, looks, and gestures which bring conviction to the hearer.

100. *What should characterize the Exhortative?*
The performer should appeal, beseech, and implore, as the case may require.

101. *What is the Slur?*
The smooth gliding of the voice in parenthetic clauses, etc.

102. *How are Emphatic words distinguished?*
By different styles of printing.

103. *How many kinds of letters are used to denote emphasis?*
Three usually.

104. *What are they?*
Italics, small capitals, and capitals.

105. *What is Antithetic emphasis?*
Same as Relative.

106. *What is Modulation?*
Variation of the voice in speaking and reading.

107. *What is Pure tone?*
A clear, flowing sound, with moderate pitch.

108. *What is the Orotund?*
Pure tone intensified.

109. *For what is it adapted?*
To express sublime and pathetic emotions.

110. *What is the Aspirated tone?*
An expulsion of breath, the words being spoken in a whisper.

111. *What is the Guttural quality?*
Deep undertone.

112. *What does it express?*
Hatred, contempt, loathing, etc.

113. *What is the Trembling tone?*
A constant waver of the voice.

114. *What does it express?*
An intense degree of suppressed excitement, or personates old age.

115. *What are Pauses?*
Suspensions of the voice in reading or speaking.

116. *How many kinds of pauses are there?*
Two.

117. *What are they?*
Grammatical and Rhetorical.

118. *What is Suspensive quantity?*
Prolongation of the voice at the end of a word without making an actual pause.

119. *What does Quantity embrace?*
Force and rate.

120. *What quality of voice is mostly used in speaking and reading?*
Pure tone.

121. *What is meant by Prose?*
All composition which is not written in verse.

122. *What are some of the varieties of Prose?*
Letters, Essays, Travels, History, and Discourses.

123. *What is a Letter as a variety of prose?*
A written communication addressed by the writer to some other person.

124. *What is an Essay?*
A written discourse on some special subject.

125. *What are Travels?*
Records of journeys.

126. *What is History?*
A record of past events.

127. *What is a Discourse?*
A performance read or spoken to an audience.

128. *Should the voice agree in style with the different varieties of prose?*
It should, and the performer should endeavor to produce the exact sentiments of the writer.

129. *What is Poetry?*
A discourse written in verse and metrical language.

130. *What is a Verse?*
A single line of metrical language.

131. *Is it correct to use the term verse in speaking of a division of prose?*
It is not.

132. *What should we call such division?*
Paragraph or Division.

133. *What is a Stanza?*
A number of metrical lines, or verses, combined according to a regular system.

134. *How many kinds of metrical language?*
Two.

135. *What are they?*
Rhyme and Blank Verse.

136. *What is Rhyme?*
That language in which the concluding syllables of the verses have a similarity of sound.

137. *How many kinds of Rhyme?*
Two.

138. *What are they?*
Perfect and imperfect.

139. *What is a Perfect rhyme?*
Where the vowels have the same sound.

140. *What is an Imperfect rhyme?*
Where the vowels have a different sound.

141. *What is Blank Verse?*
A kind of metrical language in which there is no similarity of sound.

142. *What is the Cæsura pause?*
A rhythmic pause occurring in a verse.

143. *How many rules should be observed in the use of the Cæsura?*
Three.

144. *Give Rule 1.*
The pause should be near the middle of the verse.

145. *Give Rule 2.*
It should never divide a word.

146. *Give Rule 3.*
Should not separate words from their modifiers, as adjectives from nouns, adverbs from verbs, etc.

147. *Do all verses have the Cæsura pause?*
They do if over three feet in length.

148. *What is meant by a Foot in verse?*
A certain portion of a line divided according to accent.

149. *When melody comes in contact with accent, which should yield?*
Accent.

150. *Is there any other rhythmic pause than the Cæsura?*
There is; the demi-cæsura is sometimes used.

151. *How many kinds of Poetry are there?*
Seven.

152. *What are they?*
Epic, Dramatic, Lyric, Elegiac, Didactic, Satiric and Pastoral.

153. *What is an Epic poem?*
A poetical recital of some great and heroic enterprise.

154. *Are there many Epic poems?*
There are not; most nations have one.

155. *Name the three Epics of greatest note.*
Homer's Iliad, Virgil's Æneid, and Milton's Paradise Lost.

156. *What language were these poems written in?*
The Iliad in Greek, Æneid in Latin, and Paradise Lost in English.

157. *What does the Iliad describe or narrate?*
The downfall of Troy, which was the most memorable event in the early history of the Trojans and Greeks.

158. *What does the Æneid narrate?*
The perils and labors of Æneas, who was the reputed founder of the Roman race.

159. *What does Paradise Lost describe?*
The downfall of not only the Human but of the Angelic host.

160. *What is a Dramatic poem?*
One similar in many respects to an Epic.

161. *Name some point of difference.*
Epic relates past events; the Drama represents events as taking place at the present time.

162. *Name the greatest Dramatic writer of the English.*
Shakespeare.

163. *What is a Drama called that is set to music?*
An opera.

164. *What is a Melodrama?*
A dramatic poem some parts of which are spoken and some are sung.

165. *What is Lyric Poetry?*
It is the oldest kind of poetry, and was originally intended to be sung to the accompaniment of the lyre.

166. *What are Sonnets?*
A kind of Lyric Poems.

167. *What is an Elegy?*
A poem of a mournful kind, usually celebrating the virtues of some person deceased.

168. *What is an Epitaph?*
A short Elegy inscribed on a monument, or written in praise of any one.

169. *What is a Pastoral poem?*
One that describes country life.

170. *What is a Didactic poem?*
One the aim of which is to give instruction.

171. *What is Meditative Poetry?*
A kind of Didactic poetry.

172. *Name two noted Didactic poems.*
Bryant's "Thanatopsis," and Campbell's "Pleasures of Hope."

173. *What is a Satire?*
One that holds up the follies of men to ridicule.

174. *Is a Satire personal?*
It is not.

175. *What is a Lampoon?*
A poem that attacks individuals.

176. *What is Gesture?*

Expression given to language by movements of the body, limbs, etc.

177. *What kind of Gesture is most appropriate?*
That which is natural.

178. *What attitude should be used in reading and speaking?*
Standing.

179. *Which hand should hold the book?*
The left, if possible.

180. *Should a Reader keep his eyes on the book constantly?*
He should not; but cast the eyes away from the page as often as possible.

181. *Should a gesture be made while the eyes are looking on the book?*
It should not.

182. *In what kind of language are gestures inappropriate?*
Didactic or unimpassioned discourse.

183. *Should a Speaker begin to gesticulate as soon as he begins his discourse?*
Very seldom, before he has entered fully into the discourse.

184. *How many positions are recognized for the hand when not used in gesticulating?*
Three.

185. *What are they?*
Hanging naturally at the side; resting upon the hip with the elbow thrown backward; and resting on your bosom.

186. *What are Descriptive gestures?*
Those used in describing objects.

187. *What are Significant gestures?*
Those which have special signification.

188. *Name some Significant gestures of the head.*

It drops in grief and shame, and nods in assent; shakes in dissent, and leans forward in attention.

189. *Name some Significant gestures of the eyes.*
Raised in prayer, weep in sorrow, burn in anger, and are cast on vacancy in thought.

190. *Name some of the passions of the mind.*
Love, anger, joy, sorrow, fear, and courage.

191. *What tone of voice should be used in the expression of Love?*
Soft, smooth, and languishing voice.

192. *What tone of voice should be used to express Anger?*
Strong, vehement, and elevated voice.

193. *Where is the best place to practice elocution and reading?*
In the open air, or in a well ventilated room.

194. *Should a Reader or Speaker pay strict attention to the rules of elocution?*
He should not, but study nature rather.

195. *What is the Soul of Oratory?*
Emotion.

196. *What is meant by the Compass of the voice?*
The range in which it can be properly controlled.

197. *How may the Compass of the voice be increased?*
By continued practice on a very low and very high key.

198. *Should a Reader or Speaker drink any liquid while exercising the voice?*
He should not, for it is injurious to the vocal chords.

199. *What effect does Tobacco have on the voice?*
It enfeebles the nervous system and breathing organs, and makes the voice dry, harsh, and ungovernable.

Benjamin Adams Hathaway

200. *What effect do Stimulants have on the voice?*
Irritate and inflame the vocal organs, which results in hoarseness and produces too high a key, which terminates in a squeaking tone.

201. *In faulty articulation what sounds are usually mispronounced?*
The vowel sounds of the unaccented syllables.

202. *What Consonants are often incorrectly dropped?*
The final consonants.

203. *How may distinct Articulation be acquired?*
By continued practice of the elementary sounds.

204. *What are the most prominent Elements of all words?*
The vowels.

205. *Which sounds should be practiced first?*
The vowels; as they are the most easily uttered.

206. *Can the sounds of the Consonants be given alone?*
They can by practice.

207. *What is the source of the greatest defect in Articulation?*
Improper sounding of the consonants.

208. *What kind of Inflection is generally given to words of great emphasis?*
The falling; unless the sentiment requires the rising.

209. *When is the Inflection of a question changed from the falling to the rising?*
When it is repeated or made emphatic.

210. *In the introductory part of a sentence, where the sense is incomplete, what inflection is used?*
Unless great emphasis is required, the rising should be used.

211. *The names of persons addressed in formal speech require what inflection?*
The falling should always be used in such cases.

212. *General statements require what inflection?*
The falling.

213. *For the sake of harmony, what principle should govern the reader?*
When a sentence ends with the falling inflection, the rising should precede
    it.

214. *When sentences commence with verbs, what inflection is required?*
Mostly the rising.

215. *What is meant by an Echo in reading?*
Interrogative exclamations, where the question is repeated.

216. *Give an example of Echo.*
What's the trouble? What's the trouble? trouble enough.

217. *What inflection should be given to members of sentences connected
    disjunctively?*
First member, the rising; second member, the falling.

218. *When several Emphatic words or members come together, how should
    they be inflected?*
The most emphatic, the falling; and the others the rising.

219. *What is a Simple Series in reading?*
A series of particulars that is composed of single words.

220. *What is meant by a Compound Series?*
One that is composed of clauses is called compound.

221. *What determines Accent?*
The usage of our best speakers and writers of the present.

222. *To whom does it belong to determine and record such usage?*
The Lexicographers.

223. *Are there any cases in which we can trace the reason for the accent?*
There are; in discriminating accent where it is used to determine the parts of
    speech.

224. *Do we ever have two sets of Antitheses in the same sentence?*
We do; as each member may contain an antithesis.

225. *Give an example.*
John was hurt; William escaped.

226. *How many sets of Antitheses may be used in one sentence?*
Often three; but seldom more.

227. *Should there be any difference in the tone of voice used in reading verse and prose?*
There should be a difference.

228. *What different style ought to be used?*
The monotone and rising inflection are more frequently used in verse than in prose.

229. *What is the greatest difficulty met with in reading or declaiming poetic selections?*
In giving it that measured flow which distinguishes it from prose, without falling into a continued monotone.

230. *What is a good method to break up this habit?*
Reduce the selection to prose, and deliver it in an earnest, conversational style.

231. *Why should there be a short pause at the end of each line of poetry, even where the sense does not require it?*
In order that the measure of the poem may be more perceptible to the ear.

232. *What is it that constitutes the melody of a poem?*
The pauses and accents chiefly.

233. *What rule should govern the reader in the use of pauses and accents?*
Use variety, and not make them too prominent.

234. *What tone of voice should be used in reading a Simile in poetry?*
The simile should be read in a lower tone than the rest of the passage.

235. *What, with regard to the voice, is an important object to every speaker and reader?*
The important object is to have a full, even tone of voice.

236. *What key of the voice should be most diligently improved?*
The natural key, or that which is used most.

237. *What is meant by the natural key or pitch?*
That which is peculiar to the individual, and in which he can use most easily to himself, and most agreeably to others.

238. *How can the natural tone of voice be strengthened?*
By reading and speaking as loud as possible, without suffering the voice to rise into a higher key.

239. *What is the best method of strengthening the natural key?*
By speaking and reading strong, animated passages in a small room.

240. *How may low tones be acquired?*
By continued practice in a lower key than the natural.

241. *How may a high key be acquired?*
In the same manner as a low key; by pitching the voice first a little higher than the natural, and mastering that thoroughly, then still higher and higher.

242. *What is meant by Rotundity of the voice?*
That peculiar form of tone which the Romans called "Ore rotundo," which signifies "Round mouth."

243. *In what kind of sentences is the Rotundity of the voice exemplified?*
In the hailing of vessels, and is used especially by sailors and officers.

244. *Which is the most difficult: to raise the voice to a higher pitch, or to bring it to a lower?*
The lowering of the voice is more difficult, and requires great care and practice.

245. *What is a common fault with most public speakers?*
To run the voice into too high a key, and thus weary the hearers.

246. *What is a good rule by which to govern the voice?*
To start on a key lower than the natural, and thus avoid running too high.

247. *What are the principal styles of different reading selections?*
Descriptive, Narrative, Senatorial, Moral, Didactic, Dramatic, and Amusing.

248. *What tone of voice should be used in reading a Descriptive selection?*
The ordinary, natural tone, with a careful use of emphasis.

249. *What tone of voice is best adapted to the reading of a Narration?*
The conversational tone, with as little reference to the printed page as possible.

250. *What style is the best adapted to Senatorial reading?*
An imitative style and tone, being careful in the use of the emphatic pause.

251. *What tone is best adapted to the reading of Moral and Religious selections?*
Low and moderate tone, expressing feeling and sentiment, being careful not to read too fast.

252. *What style is best adapted to Didactic reading?*
That peculiar style which is best adapted to impart instruction, laying special stress on the important idea.

253. *What style and tone are best adapted to the reading of Dramatic selections?*
A style and tone which are entirely imitative in character.

254. *What tone or character of voice is best suited to the rendering of Amusing selections?*
That which will bring out the mirthful sentiment, to the exclusion of all rules for accent, emphasis, etc.

255. *Should all persons use the same tones of voice and style in reading selections?*

They should not; as individuals are differently constituted, so they have different ways of expressing their ideas and sentiments.

CPSIA information can be obtained
at www.ICGtesting.com
Printed in the USA
LVHW062234210723
753033LV00008B/618